Ending in Planes

2013 Noemi Press Poetry Award Winner

Ending in Planes

Ruth Ellen Kocher

Noemi Press

Noemi Press
P.O. Box 1330
Mesilla Park, NM 88047
www.noemipress.org

Cover design by Douglas Kearney
Interior design by Mo Fiorella
Author photo by Patricia Colleen Murphy

Library of Congress Cataloging-in-Publication Data

Kocher, Ruth Ellen, 1965-
[Poems. Selections]
Ending in planes / by Ruth Ellen Kocher. -- First edition.
pages cm
Summary: "Original collection of poetry" -- Provided by publisher.
ISBN 978-1-934819-36-4 (alk. paper) -- ISBN 1-934819-36-0 (alk. paper)
I. Title.
PS3561.O313A6 2014
811'.54--dc23

Acknowledgements

Thank you to the journals in which the following poems appear and those editors willing to gamble on a long poem: "Sequence Ending in Tides," *Bone Bouquet*; all sections of "Sequence Ending in Desire," *Phantom Limb*; "Beauty is No Abstract Thought," *TitMouse*; "When You Say Grotesque," *The Medulla Review*; "string theory," *Blackbird*; "Death and Petunias," *Diode*; "Cycle," *Torch*; earlier version as "Insomnia Cycle 42," *American Letters and Commentary 22*; "Two," *The Enemy*; and "Sequence Ending in Planes," *Dreginald*. I want to extend special thanks to Douglas Kearney both for the cover design of this book and his faith, which inspired me to greater faith. I want to also thank the editorial staff at Noemi Press for their collaborative and gallant efforts to exact the visual character of this project. Thank you to good friends and confidantes whose conversations helped to solidify moments in these poems, Arline and Ed Dowling, Mary Gannon, Wendy S. Walters, Tyehimba Jess, Ross Gay, Duriel Estelle Harris, Adrian Matejka and Krista Franklin. Thank you to my Cave Canem retreat family, especially Alison Meyers, Amanda Johnson, Marcus Wicker, Sami Schalk, Darrel Alejandro Holnes, Hafizah Geter, Carl Phillips, Colleen J. McElroy, Claudia Rankine, Toi Derricotte, Cornelius Eady, Robin Coste Lewis, Brian Francis, and Ashley Tolliver. I send out a special thanks to my Creative Writing Program colleagues, in particular, Julie Carr and Noah Eli Gordon, and to my many many talented students. I'd like to also cite texts to which I've responded or from which I've borrowed either conceptually or by content: Gilles Deleuze, *Difference and Repetition*, translated by Paul Patton; Ross Gay, *Against Which*; Edouard Glissant, *Poetics of Relation*, translated by Betsy Wing; Beckian Fritz Goldberg, "Refugees," from *Never Be The Horse*; David Orr, "On Poetry: Dream Logic," *The New York Times*; and David Yezzi, "The Dramatic Element: On the Social Muse," *The New Criterion*.

I dedicate this book to my parents and family, especially my daughter Kaylee, and my great one, Paul Smith.

Table of Contents

"There was never any more inception than there is now ..."

WALT WHITMAN

Death and Petunias

A woman digs a hole for roots flowering purple
This is how Death begins

And of course The love poem which no one reads anymore The kind of poem which says *yellow* Says *pink* Says *orange* Says

I hate you

Hate cannot bare this when The love Poem throws up a sharp hue Hue is a word Death uses when talking about a typical day
gathering The helix of purple flowers

In her arms Which are not flowers Are stop signs
open-eyed starry Are Neighbors Children just heard not seen

In time In Time

The woman would gather Latin in her arms but
Petunia is always *petunia*

Death knows this failure that lurks in botany So soothes her Death says *darling* Death says *poem* Death says *Love We are The same*

She Admits She Dreams of Grass

A morning can be all about earth
and the epistles that spring from it.

Scene 6: The day is unremarkable. Magnolia
takes up flourishing in usual lushness.

it is summer it is summer it is summer
Window squares reflect crosswalk-lines

interrupt sky upon blue sky upon blue

Scene 6: The smell   somehow undone   first picked
green   yes   but familiar to the body that takes it
accords it light in a way

most opaque   sifted
turned out

moss creek on her breath.
Epilogue:

Sequence Ending in Desire

i

I can't make the theology of my mouth into any beginning

Do you know syllable-smooth-bellied-fine-with-platitudes (joy sounds like this) fails in the way a sentence finds inevitable stop   The come-on

It ends Not badly It falls off the way morning snow slips noon into mud hardly seen turning this to that

Say my name only in marigolds Tell the next The next only sweet pea My Lips My sometimes My cut grass

Maybe I call once hear the background laugh (and she laughs)
The peonies happy its all done But the finches and sunlight And summer lilies (we saw blinding the orange rim of the roads)

You come sound You come blind note You come never before

Say I want nothing Want nothing meaning all meaning not larks not eclipse not every pear which everyone easily forgets (and the dead tree and the bear and the sky turned red)

The articles of nothing make everything we have (the flowers   the blue cups   The smell of sea though there was none)

The articles of everything make no longer as in No longer can I not imagine the end

You butter your bread You wash the clothes The hum reminds you of something The not which is there The glass blind light or blinding Nothing never ends

ii

Blue is less mortal Not the least blue
the ocean will not bare Not blue swallowing you whole

Any joy deliberate as joy keeps itself from blue and purpose
Do not paint me more color than waves.

Say you love me this way Less than a great epiphany

Almost more mortal than blue can I go away like the blink you imagine by forgetting Love me like this Just remembered now

What I really want to say Your coffee is bitter The towels frayed The petunias need watering

Joy let's say the clear air and hands in your pockets keeps from blue and purpose As though a cliff says *fall* A wind says *hiss*

Do not think of the painter this way He painted Not my face
I want to say Do not think of the painter and think tangerine Do not

think limp room Orange flourish Sky crack
Hate me in the way you hate a beautiful thought

Silver bellied sheen You paint what you know to be true You are not hungry but bare me as blue the ocean cannot

You love me dank Moist night My heart no willow pond Water
coming and going and sounding The rush we prefer to say brook

iii

The nightingale says You have made too much of my name Go away Close the window The breeze doesn't care

Here's what we know You've figured us out singing through the dark in trees that know no better than to allow us Trees tired of all the racket

and Romance which does nothing for birds either Don't get cocky   It's not our wisdom Ringed swoop Be what I want you to want to be

I have to say even as I'm showering A knocked down woman is pathetic to love you It's all been talked about so much

I speak like this supposing you hear more than What's his name? It's a dance-off Really Not your line Like everything You make it yours

Someone cares because the Word has nothing of us without pause If you listened you would understand The shell and the ear is a story we tell our children Silence discovers us in this way

I have many You should know The way I kiss them all goodbye.

Not your lonely Lonely as a moment can never choose Hear the bird all night

That pause Not a tender slip Not nudge Because fucking just has to be done Yes I said it not beautiful as swans or geese geese or herons

Be what I want before you go When I forget you As I forget you I will forget you Mostly silent The trees love us for this and even the us you imagine

Swans and herons have no say You measure the extent The cliché and hollow Nothing forgives a singular function Swans like the others say Go away

iv

I forgot again to name the sky

A man with his arm pulled back That fist That guy will cough only dust Say even orbits of Embers

Waiting for the sound of shattering fills the quiet spaces we anticipate losing

You believe me I have lied I have not forgotten to name the sky a desolate ruined thing

Ember knows even paper napkins and paper covered
straws which you are always given whether you need them or not Billboards of course Landscape of glitches

Not a thing to be in the world But worlds too large to speak You cannot speak a tree or the word itself A tree cannot be what we call it

You cannot change the billboards or the cows that gather between them You can change I hate that you love me is enough

Forget something burns You imagine coffee without cream Oatmeal Not name A word that gives you up Never this Nor the sound of leaving a room

Do you forget we are talking about fire and the way you've been gone

I've told you what I've told you is not believable enough to escape

Do not believe the freeways either
The freeways cough with you so you're not alone

Your sediment Your ditch Not particularly rare A burnt spot on the rug not undone

v

Sometimes you love a fist

Sometimes you need a man to come down on you like trees roughed up by a storm Sometimes you like it but don't say so

Not to the door Not to the window nor the splintered porch You don't say sometimes You pity that you're loved

A first life stabs you The bright red of fire which darkens so quickly The cut begs to tell us What's true

I wanted your beautiful torso Its stretch Its beautiful face Its doorway I wanted your Honey yes Your be good Your goodnight I wanted you're mine I wanted you're mine You're mine and I own you

The clover said *He is not* and it happens that the tulips didn't notice The water barely resisted with cobalt blue which means *be good for a woman* But cobalt most often lies

Listen You may hate how the sky sounds But the bed was never yours The gardenias kept growing indiscernibly red As all desire does

In the dark My back says I am not afraid of you

The whole body never knows what the parts do A heart can tangle in cat's claw Which is yellow flowers which is clutching a wall Which is I will not let you go

All you had to say All you had to say is The tomatoes ripe you would have loved to see

When you lose a thing you love it more of course Though a lost thing may mean swindle Mean right hook Slow cook The send it while you have it Lonesome anyway

The second life excuses you from the stupid ache in your chest

I only hate your hands

vi

Where a thing begins has to do with unraveling

You would not let me be on my knees You dabbed my shin with gauze You made the bed as soon as you rose You ate my oatmeal without sugar You bought cigars you didn't smoke even outside You shoveled the deck when it snowed in April You were timid about the closet and hanging your clothes You loved my friends You drove me everywhere You loved my flowers You took pictures of my flowers You tapped out syllables on my back You fixed my hair You did not walk around naked You looked like a boy in your towel You looked naked in your towel You slept in the same position every night You watched me sleep You told me to go to bed and that was fine You said lay on my chest You said you're tired You're hungry You should eat You should sleep You should walk You should get the mail You should shop now You should cook now You should sleep The bed felt warm when I waited for you I asked you when I should sleep

If you spoke as the first time speaking I would want to not want you again

The best part of heartbreak is the matter of being alive The park seems less quiet Everything gets in your way I want most for you to be a monster The beginning is hardest to remember The end being greedy for what it wants

That anywhere love can be less abstract becomes a burden the shoulders bear instead of the heart Not like a load of wood Not a sack Burden like the weight of someone who stills you by holding As someone who would lay himself on your back

The sky has seemed to need a name called What happens when the blue falls As though blue could keep me without your hands As though your hands understood why a vowel like "a" sounds like yellow in a mind like mine Because you held that sweet pear for a moment longer And I ate it out of your hand Because it was not the first sweet in the palm of your hand and not the first sweet you fed me

Good Morning I told you I'd make it right This is me Early morning Three hours of sleep Maybe four But I'm here and I'm happy The sun's shining and I'm happy Speaking to you I told you Here's my morning Here's my kiss

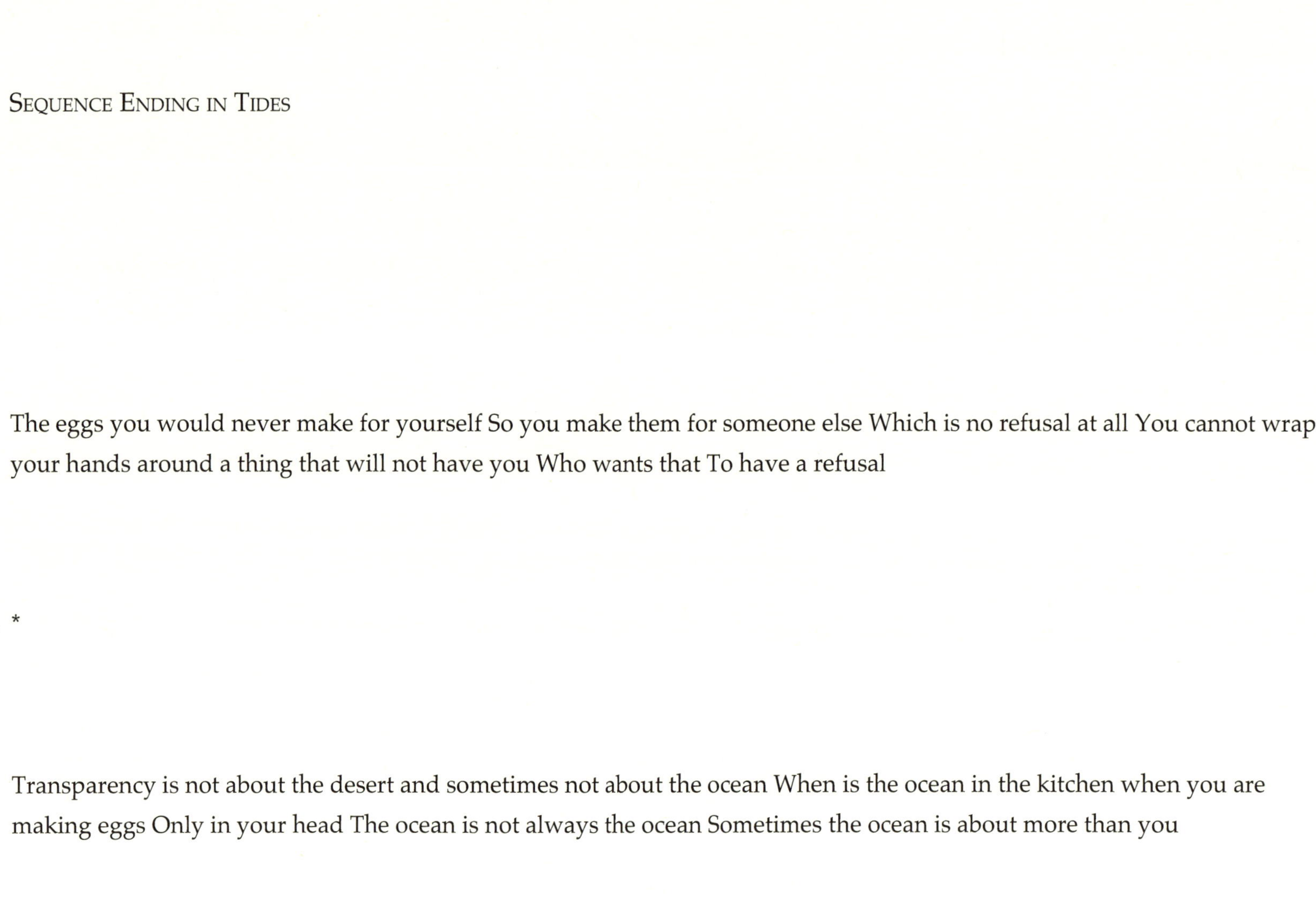

Sequence Ending in Tides

The eggs you would never make for yourself So you make them for someone else Which is no refusal at all You cannot wrap your hands around a thing that will not have you Who wants that To have a refusal

*

Transparency is not about the desert and sometimes not about the ocean When is the ocean in the kitchen when you are making eggs Only in your head The ocean is not always the ocean Sometimes the ocean is about more than you

Forget about any of these things not part of you in any way Today or tomorrow You will come back to a smell and forget things not in your hands Onions Parsley Butter cooking you remember also as only one thing

*

Without speaking of your childhood Which is the same as anyone else's Not so much remembered as tacked down Without your childhood you wanted nothing from the way you wake up in the morning the same way everyday A childhood would not want everyday like this

Someone smells cooking in the kitchen Remembers a split field in front of him and pigs squealing somewhere down a dirt road Chickens with pigs A barn so he couldn't breathe at all

*

In your kitchen A childhood has a blue bike and a scar inside someone's thigh Your own thigh you realize opening a cupboard Someone might say no one needs to know this so This stays blank Who we are means so much more now When I am telling And you are listening easily Out of habit The way you would look for salt on the shelf

*

You think of a man selling vacuums from a binder with pictures in cellophane the way you remember also cigarette smoke While cooking Reaching for salt and then pepper The ocean wants none of this trying to hold on

In another room you come home to someone who waits and smells eggs And the ocean off a cliff You talk about it sometimes An island with a name you can't remember You tell people about the island As though it's not true

*

You always return to the same L-shaped room The same and you love this As anyone could The sound outside the door day and night

Insomnia For The Wet Horses

I want to go fishing I want the fish to have something to say I want the trees to be pissed off I want the trees to say *Hey you Hey you Scat*

Who are you on a rock? Who are you on a boat? Who are you at the cafe counter in Sevilla? You ask the man Are the goats happy? Are the goats happy? He points to the cheese

Sunflowers do not know where not to go Give them a field and they have a field which becomes not a field but sunflower North are olives North further sunflowers And so on

Trains inhabit the sleep of women sleeping in their beds because trains are filled with women dreaming somewhere besides their beds The dreams which are hard to talk about because everyone knows them The dream The dream The dream so done so used so easy-reach The dreams cannot forget themselves and so don't go away

When he points to the cheese I imagine hay and horses in dense rain which I do not tell you

When I ask who you are on a boat I mean for you to answer me When I want to fish I do When you intend to do something he said When you intend then you always fail I can't accept what you mean if I can't mean for you to answer me

You have gone from there to here Not a vague reference to inner narrative You are here too We are vague together We are on a boat We are in a shop asking the price of blue asking the time of day Nodding Smiling

Thorn yourself over there where the walk through berries is worth it No that's only a dream How do you say dream when you're trying to avoid cliché? Just berries Just walking

The goats were happy the man told you And the Hay And the rain Though his language you didn't understand

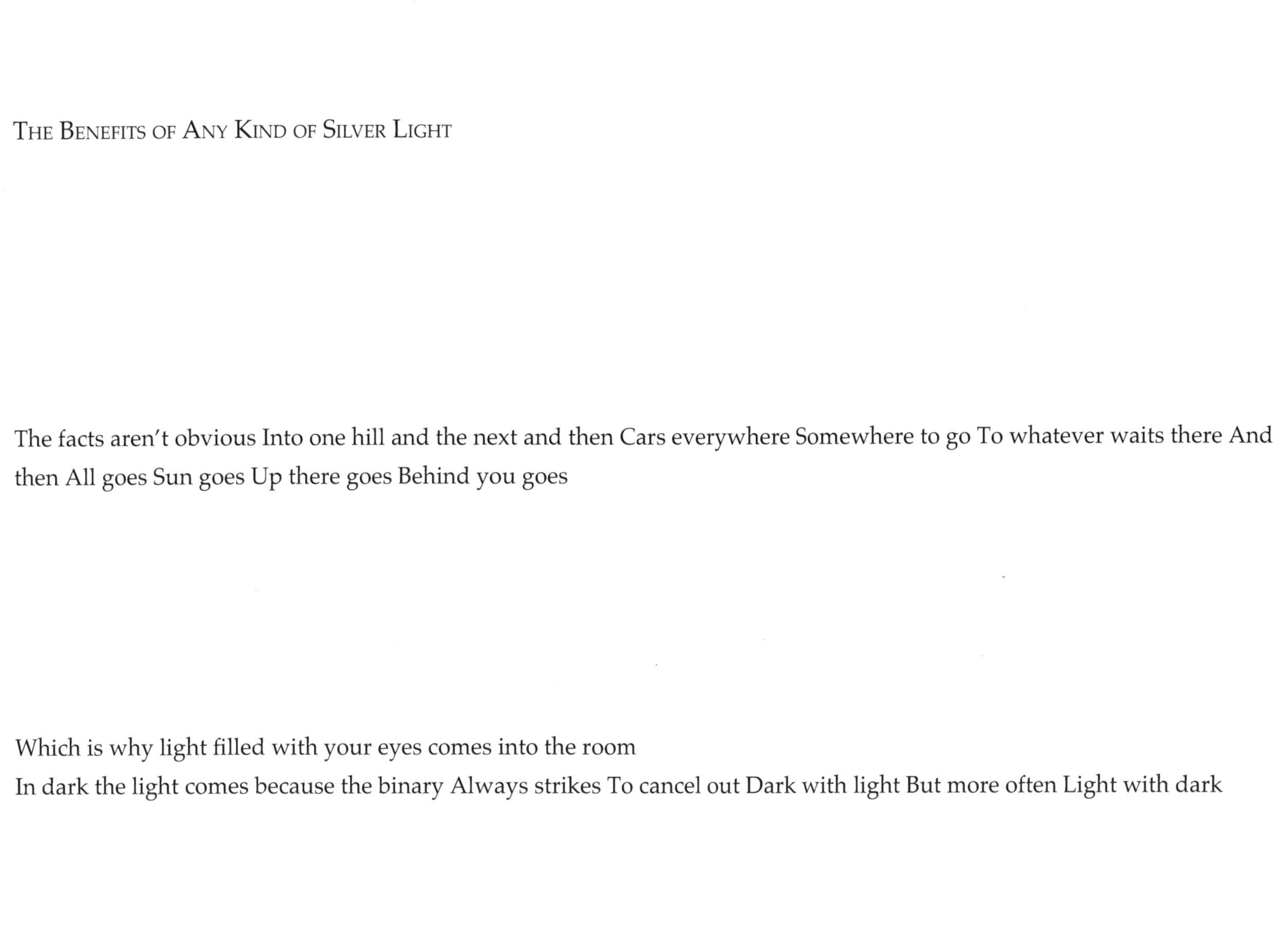

The Benefits of Any Kind of Silver Light

The facts aren't obvious Into one hill and the next and then Cars everywhere Somewhere to go To whatever waits there And then All goes Sun goes Up there goes Behind you goes

Which is why light filled with your eyes comes into the room
In dark the light comes because the binary Always strikes To cancel out Dark with light But more often Light with dark

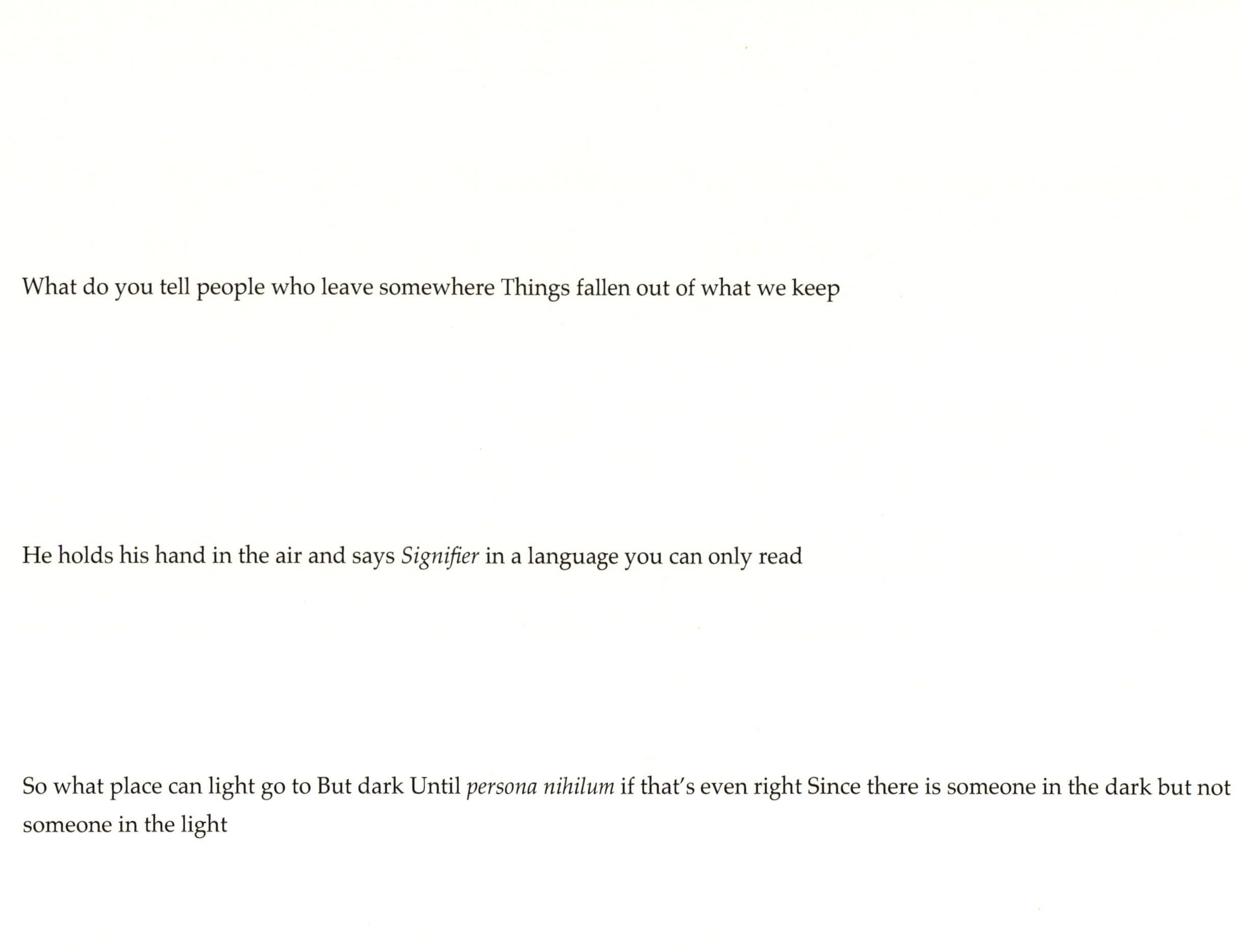

What do you tell people who leave somewhere Things fallen out of what we keep

He holds his hand in the air and says *Signifier* in a language you can only read

So what place can light go to But dark Until *persona nihilum* if that's even right Since there is someone in the dark but not someone in the light

Thinking about the light means you think about eclipse Which wants another night A scheduled night that people talk about weeks in advance Are you watching they ask each other each time Eclipse wants another night Not this one A darker night like Neruda's dark things Dark things which are loved

The eclipse you wander into A constellation you didn't learn in high school but Homer you stole later Homer stands in the silver light also The window gives up Not Homer by light

You've read about the way you hear the way you speak Even though to speak prefigures your voice Not your utterance and Utterance is most useful for music that obscures music unless you take time unless you take time Because

T begs an extra moment and an extra moment *T* begs for To be endless *Temecula Torrential Tectonic Tally* You've talked about this all before To everyone

David Yezzi says the lyric voice is Eliot's second voice (the poet talking to an audience) is the third voice (characters talking to each other)

Or the light says to you Not anyone else To you as though you will answer *Come back We're waiting to talk liquid We're ready to talk star*

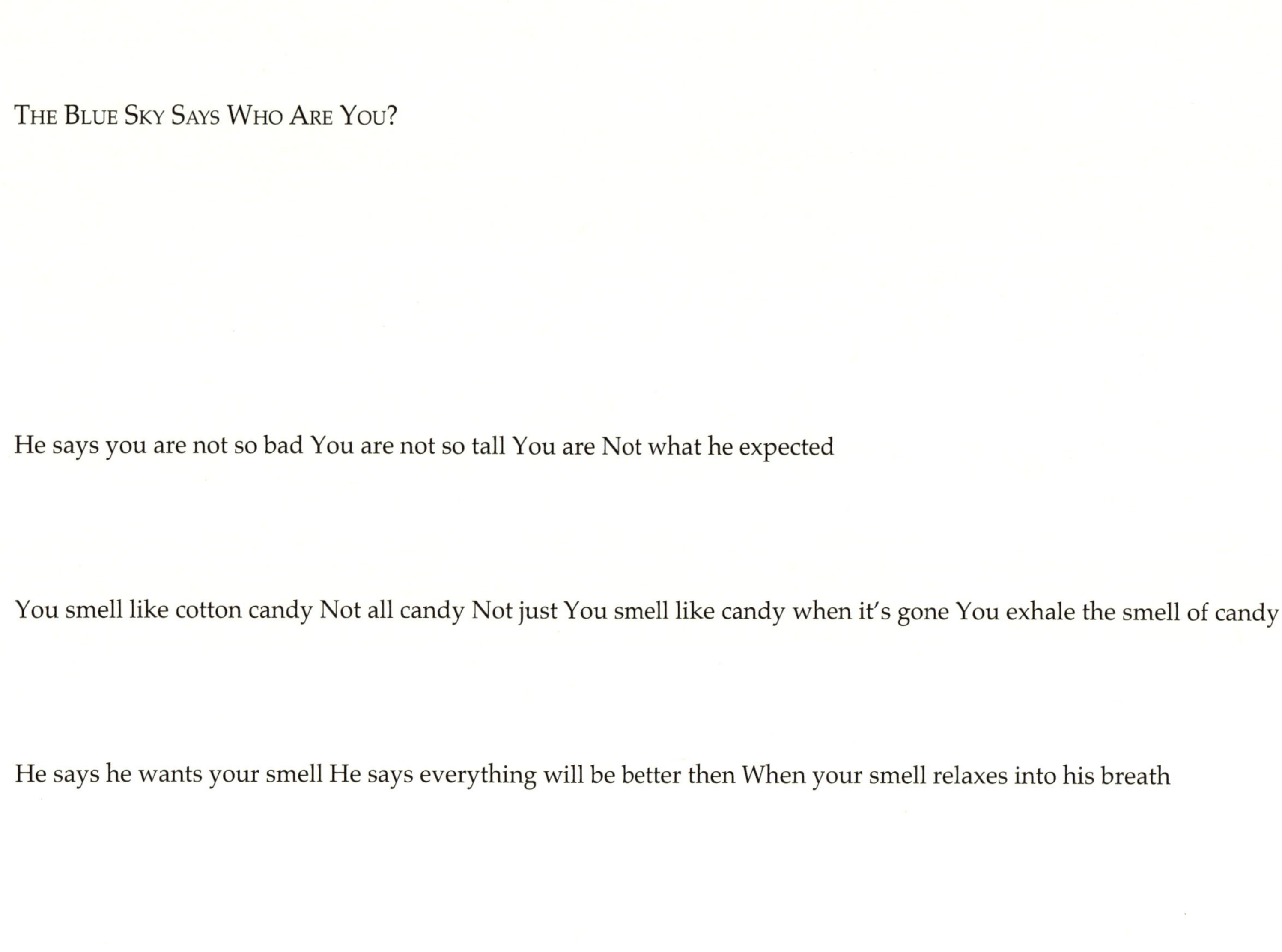

The Blue Sky Says Who Are You?

He says you are not so bad You are not so tall You are Not what he expected

You smell like cotton candy Not all candy Not just You smell like candy when it's gone You exhale the smell of candy

He says he wants your smell He says everything will be better then When your smell relaxes into his breath

You are Not what he expected Not so tall Pretty for who you are

He says all of this simply snapping his fingers You are to be You be what was Like All transitive

He says

The grammar of cloud will not say The grammar of a mountain is a dash – And never ends

He has given up lakes He has gone to The sea The sea smells opposite of everything else Hollow

You are not what stays here candy-breath You are not what He expected.

Making a Scene

[Cut]

What you have you have
Be sure to check out what your favorite becomes
[Pause]
The street is not quiet

Wet is a sound also
[Softly]

Our talk does not mean
My doorknob or your doorknob
Or anything greater

Not about what you might imagine
To be a leaf

Not a leaf   what you call it
Accents are the ghost of a language
A country that's died in a mouth
I don't know what else to say
Next door someone says this to someone
younger while All mulch under
the window Under the trees
He's wearing a pink shirt tucked behind a black belt
The older What you call
(All outside full of What appears
four benches One table)
call it Arbitrary

Scene 4:

The smallest things are sleeping

Where too many things exist to Tell
Someone Or you might say
Anyone The buildings
Full of not enough
Full of the green circle of things

About which (who said?) is a title
[light should seem morning dim]

you nor I know
All too many
too many

To hear

[Enter]

[Enter]
Now everything to
the Sleeping belongs

Say it to the sky
In the way no one can say
It is familiar or done

Sand is boring   hello
Hello hello you would say
Each person passing
On a boring beach

Common where the
Sea cannot sustain An action
and so Become pond

Under study the walls
The curtains

You receive a letter that says Allegory
Is dead This is a question the letter
wants you to answer as though it is not a question
but an answer Not in a post-
lapsarian autumn yellow dusk hour
car lights beginnings and endings
Sort of way though They is
An allegory Not unlike
You are an allegory

Half notes Head to toe

A flute always brings

The piano   the language
Of instruments like

That Baldwin piece when the narrator
Finally hears The brother speaking
A quiz on breath and touch

The piano plays too long

What information do you need to know
You can't already know to touch

Just spine and keys
[someone's watching]

And know breath

Touch things Only to know touch

Here's why

Trees nowhere inside of him
as unimportant as Which tree
Where

Here he rises out of the soil
Monster Big like a comic book

All rock

Nothing grows there

Don't you dare lie to me
Music begins

He's seen that look many times
And the music becomes louder.

C'mon Piano. A neighbor comes.
Next week comes A yard of course

Expect roses The porch
You should imagine
The way houses look
And   gutters

Before it ends
the woodwinds return
all but the "it" Which is the oboe

[scene]

You must have a child
To understand
Tasting being so personal

Salt especially and sugar

Sour everyone understands The way you think is the way
We all think:
Right here: [three coats isn't enough unless
 it dries I need to remember before I finish]
this *theory of mind* in children may be mistaken
for the way we think to understand the way we
think You to understand – What I know Everyone
knows

Right here: I can't keep myself out of it
It's maybe a lack of the dramatic the essay Yezzi talks about Failing language as language does Do you know The essay says the essay fails No Éduoard Glissant in any of the essays lacking A dramatic and So failing

Then to close things
Tell me just one thing I need to know about you
Just one thing

From now on where are we headed?
The music changes. You can only hear
As if you could actually hear
risk The sound of People dancing is Not
the best thing to say

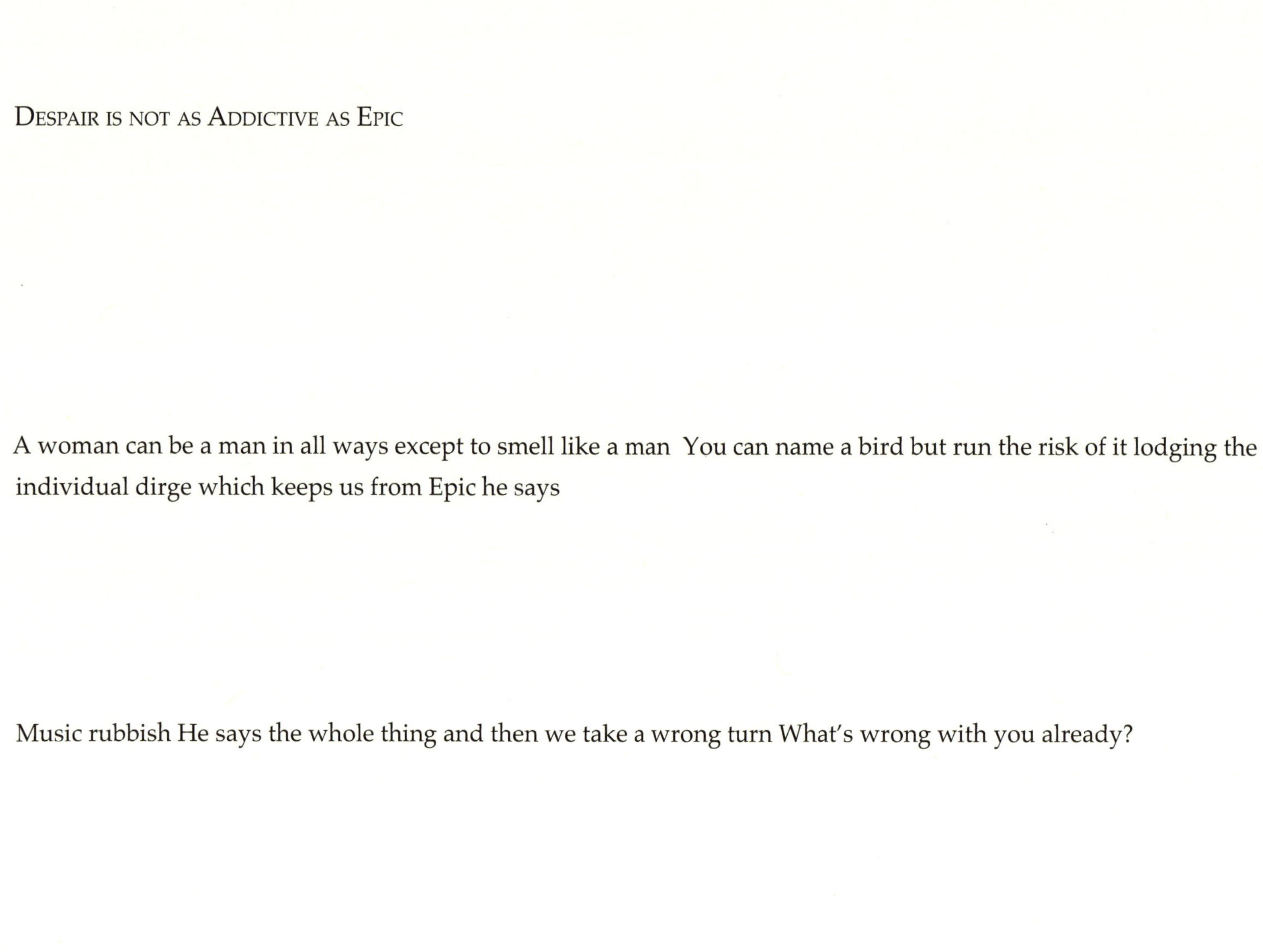

Despair is not as Addictive as Epic

A woman can be a man in all ways except to smell like a man You can name a bird but run the risk of it lodging the individual dirge which keeps us from Epic he says

Music rubbish He says the whole thing and then we take a wrong turn What's wrong with you already?

To smell like a man can only be realized by a woman smelling a man More than any other way that any other thing can smell the scapula Which knits itself to its other

The chest rises [Men smell other men in this way and know always the bristle but seldom say so] [Women smell women in this way and find themselves there]

One day begins She says the Larks are snarky thinking that Sound belongs to them The next day they are not Larks but Nightingales

Do not imagine Nightingales are Epic except to say everyone uses them knowing they say something Again and again And so use them again and again

Nightingales have made themselves available to Despair They are on the make They are for all intensive purposes common-law partners [Men and women smell themselves and others]

The Nightingales cannot say anything useful about Addiction or Despair having forgotten encounter [Women encounter men and also women and Men encounter in this way also] [Somewhere within the encounter of smell is a feeble flip of the heart]

You might think easy So the bird is alone in the wind Or the bird and other birds are alone as birds are collectively alone in the wind

Or the bird should have a name Not nightingale Not bird Ruby-throat Redwing Kingfisher

And what follows is disappointment that birds cannot be the same thing again and again You wish for something else to be alone in the wind

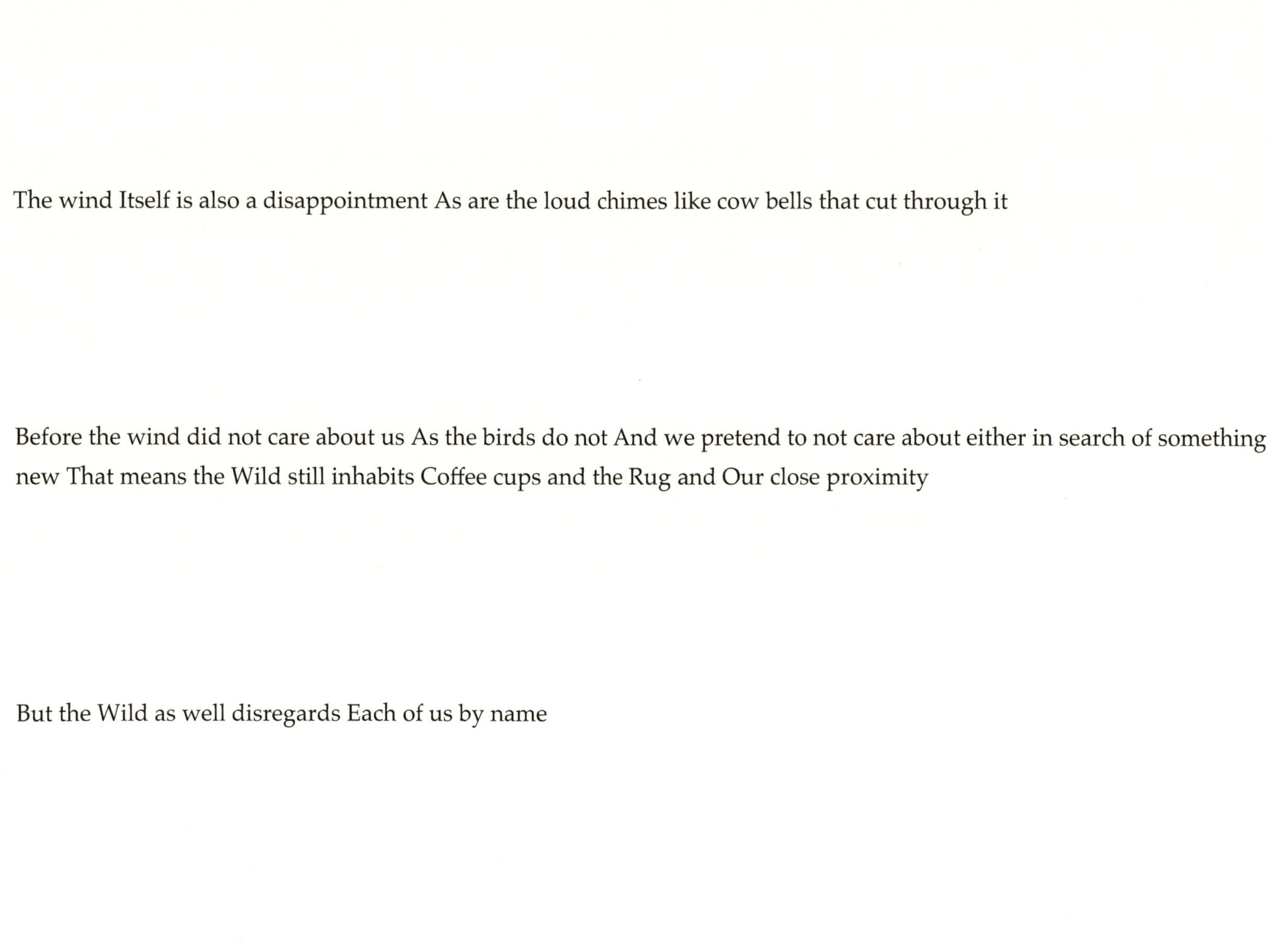

The wind Itself is also a disappointment As are the loud chimes like cow bells that cut through it

Before the wind did not care about us As the birds do not And we pretend to not care about either in search of something new That means the Wild still inhabits Coffee cups and the Rug and Our close proximity

But the Wild as well disregards Each of us by name

Addiction comes only as we are civilized Civil and concrete and Boredom and aluminum siding Not marble Thinking it can play Wild if it puts on a hat If it dances If it imagines purple and delights you

Addiction smells Despair and thinks as much about a man as a woman thinks about a woman or a man and as much as a man cannot help but think about another man

Addiction cannot help but thinking of the world this way You do not need to know what this is Addiction thinks of the world and does not see birds as birds don't see us

Despair loves all Which is every one thing Everywhere Despair is the second row seat who claps too long Wants to be watched Hopes you turn around Despair winks at the stage Only bright lights keep it invisible

Two

He still looks for his face Which she didn't imagine Or could not find Or forgot and she imagined something else As a yarn caught her eye As a bus did not come As an understanding between two people One has a red jacket The other crosses his arms

He looks for his face which should be everywhere He should be someplace Where she finds him Regardless of where he walks Back if she remembered Storage units go unclaimed And the papers And the mail Where is he at?

Stop looking Go away The great valley too Her puzzle on the table undone Leaf on the glass She looks everywhere There is no face she says to the frozen bush The foot steps she's never seen It's not as though a villain suddenly appears and tells us what to not and then What to do

It's not as though the beta fish want to fight The color lets them which is why every surface cannot have them They stay in rows When the rows are broken the fish die

Water had them No plants No face No way to find Where she misplaced the way she looks for him If he can find what she doesn't imagine He could see small clips and baskets everywhere The way everything she can't find she organizes

Sleeping remains an option Behind her *Stop rolling my egg down the hill* The commercials don't always have anything to do with what's on She watches because There is often music In music She wouldn't look for anything

string theory

it was not your sun. it was not your sweat

your hand nor breath nor talk again i think it was a verse

it was not fast food nor never again will the bliss not

your idea and it wasn't. not one of them. her or her

or her. none of them asked you if you wanted back.

my sky is my sky and you do not share it although

i know your sky well. it has nothing to do with gravity.

it does not subscribe to the typical physics of corn rows.

the buildings with their dreamy steel tits will never touch it.

would your sky if it called you would you hear your name.

it is true that 'to be' is a very weak verb   even though
it is true there were raspberries in the refrigerator.
it is true there were mice in the closet   and in the rice.
it is true that 'to be' cannot mean to mean more than it is
and to be as much is to be beyond – what   is it true?

i have been thinking about how nothing has happened
the way we remember it happening   and how what we
remember   is only ours. you never said yes in the way
i remember. your hands did not mean what i thought   either.
i thought not one thing your hands have agreed to remember.

you're so absent – from me. is this

what you meant in the Thai restaurant in Boston –

how the bird calls. the bird calls. the bird calls.

the bird calls   and nothing answers .

nothing calls for the bird. so the bird goes away

Cycle

When someone says the Garden of Eden was in Missouri you are not supposed to laugh And the compulsion to laugh says something about the body map of arteries through the center regions of your body where the soul lives in parts and what the soul thinks of the Garden of Eden or Missouri or both or the voice that let go a sincere ridicule perhaps even expectedly His shirt short sleeved button up the kind of beige that looks yellow and inside of himself he sits sure There is no way for the soul in each of its parts to not respond to Missouri and the Mississippi and the bridges that let people drive their silver vans in the sun of the other side There is no way the water tower in the middle of the river is not filled with ghosts who are cousins to souls and who respond to everything who become only earth and air who are filled with atmospheres we don't think to remember The Garden of Eden smells like cows and horse shit then it follows and river mud and ice storms which have only the smell that the streets give them Missouri is Africa because everyone knows we started there We sleepwalked there We searched for gates We found yards of fabric for business wear We walked our small dogs and had clean nails The fan The fan The fan Out of Africa never made an impression except for the fans and the yards of fabric draped over the beds in what we see as romantic deliberately thrown into the contrariness of use The air has been so long below the atmosphere it has forgotten rain The ghosts don't understand Missouri The fall they don't remember The bridges either

Doctrine of Release

i.

Vector: a moment worth remembering
traffic light   orange poppies choking a field.

ii.

Gravity: any closed conducting path   the way pines
lean as the day goes on   the earth asking them back.

iii.

Resistance: coconut popsicles bought on your own. A lover.
Palm trees. You are lost. You are lost. You are lost.

iv.

Fundamental Constants: god / God / Jesus / Buddha. The eye behind you. Landlord has a key. Housing and Urban Development.

v.

Coordinate Systems: magnitude and direction
the yolk of an egg   its simple task   exposed.

vi.

Potential: rain meets and releases earth.
A flirtatious turn of marigold at 5 a.m.

vii.

Radiation: begin with an oar and find a boat   a boat
and a pond   a pond and a wood   a wood and a mountain.

viii.

Friction: movement inhibited. Burnt patches
of the dead country in rows of singed grasses.

ix.

Momentum: slug   roach   maggot   moth
beetle   worm   lice.

x.

Impulse: equal to the difference of momentum   a body
at two instances. Collision. We   moving with.

Beauty is No Abstract Thought

Someone said a lightening bolt opened the earth
How it is then we find blue rock Something like blue

Can be imagined coming from both Above and Below

I do not understand money I understand the pretty
seconds Tick tick Time not but a Pink
sweater Draws every hand toward it wanting to touch

You cannot forget for a moment the bird is a rock
The blue feathers take sun four colors each describable

But for some close cousin: Cerulean Ochre Teal Green

Understand tanzanite These are almost gone Call now

The miners are sweet hard workers They cannot always
Run the air tanks Fuel costs so much I'm proud of selling

A dead starfish so accidentally mistakes a beauty We love it
Draw it We ink our arms to it Shame is no abstract thought

Don't pulse Don't one arm ebb thinking toward another

Mounting

In a dead country The room is simple As anyone knows who has seen it The scene she cannot make simply You can try to make yellow walls less yellow But the wall is the wall

Nothing to hang nor nothing ready to hang and so the windows again again A dog with silver sunglasses A storyboard in a canyon Who she is no one knows but she

reads a book sideways to the camera cameo Lorraine Hansberry Hello Monkey family Mirror Josephine Baker Krista again and again collage collage and language no one can speak under ochre The closet keeps coal processing in the dark Blue

Flame knocked out windows Ink And so it changes Snow Quickly All of this is easy to remember if she Makes it into a room even though No voice tells her

The cantaloupe wasn't ripe Romaine pink at the base What inside means as She told him and He told her back Both braced in Alone can be a bad guest Alone scratches all the time Picks her toes

Upstairs and downstairs the same The crooked woman walking Bob not the cat further but the dog In the upstairs room The wall and Estrella which is an old 45 record player and Her lovely feet salvaged She recalls from a chain link fence in Granada A black frame makes it legitimate art Lorca's shut doors and windows The green shudders and many orange trees Mirror Mounting squares but Nothing to hang The desk downstairs where

her milk glass Used and left Nothing nor nothing ready and so the windows the silver She remembers looking in the window Lorca's desk held a pen only No

canyon – no milk glass The downstairs and the Upstairs she calls her own are actually different Tree line The joggers cross by bridge Quickly it changes like now as He walks in snow She will always imagine him far away Inside where she stays

When She finds instead Green

the risk in saying I do not love you
charms its way into this poem

This brown poem which I cannot say is brown which I cannot say is white Not white is the color of The said not had As if apples had fallen from your hands

As though apples have somewhere to go
Everywhere you forget yourself

too many shoes… too many oceans… too many
… matches and horses and odometers

When you imagine the trees hover menacing you are right
About the trees and The apples and the filth that was white

The risk in Saying I do not love you Charms a hole into this poem
Filthy mountain filthy road filthy wire Filthy cloud filthy breath filthy stars

…too many paintings of trees… too many
salons and pennies… too much velvet …

The risk in saying I do not charms Do not into
do Not as you've said do not And said do not again

I do not mean to confuse you I do not want you to not understand Do not do Do not say Do not the apples fall from your hands

When you are finished with me When you are finished The trees
Look down menacing The earth which I always come back to

And leave again Say you understand Say the Rhetoric of cliff
Means you will leave Say what you mean as if to grass

Old broad Old rock Old tit of trees
Go Away

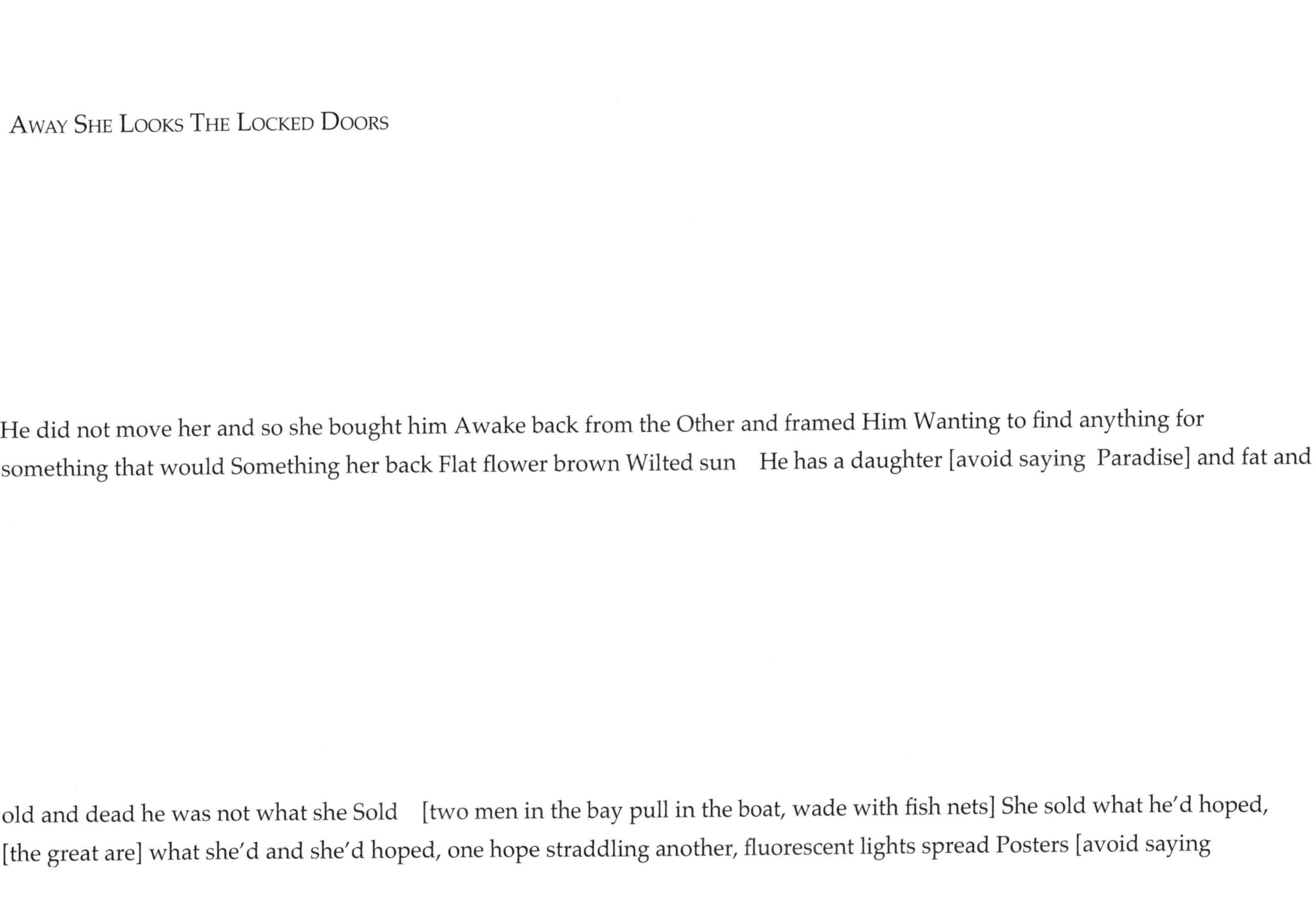

Away She Looks The Locked Doors

He did not move her and so she bought him Awake back from the Other and framed Him Wanting to find anything for something that would Something her back Flat flower brown Wilted sun He has a daughter [avoid saying Paradise] and fat and

old and dead he was not what she Sold [two men in the bay pull in the boat, wade with fish nets] She sold what he'd hoped, [the great are] what she'd and she'd hoped, one hope straddling another, fluorescent lights spread Posters [avoid saying

Paradise] [two men with fish nets] She imagined were genius Her father at the window and gone Left to her No piece [the great are] can she find in wilted flowers or weeks which do not even have good shape or composition and in muddy not

peaked into Saint Martin's technicolor The only right way to say everything [People wait] He is gone though it is a dated way to say absence and Something made instead of [avoid saying Duchamp] The picture she thinks died not about her and with him her father [two men wade with fish nets] And she whose Father died there Looks for as though [The People wait] [wade with fishnets] Maybe he'll water flowers and also a mule will come The fence stands near the house near the reason near the dumb heart

The house awful humid so scorpions come in [avoid saying Paradise] He hated her Perhaps [avoid saying] him Dead [the great are] fat and not yet Famous though the Gallery sold She is Closed on Sundays but open the rest [People wait] How stupid We are the same She thinks Death where she knows only rot and compost Not pleading see The woman cannot eat the poster [two men wade with fish nets] The poster has nothing too

another initiative in cahoots with the furthest gray wall When a night Comes and eclipse but not So much they are what [People wait] then Wait for But the moon which No one talks about Dark and the wall and the dull image of paper will go away no trace Make another way   Above and Below cancel out Blue or one breath relaxing into another until Both forget More than just walking just berries on the way to the car and jasmine Which is not fit for a poem and a fence that keeps out everything

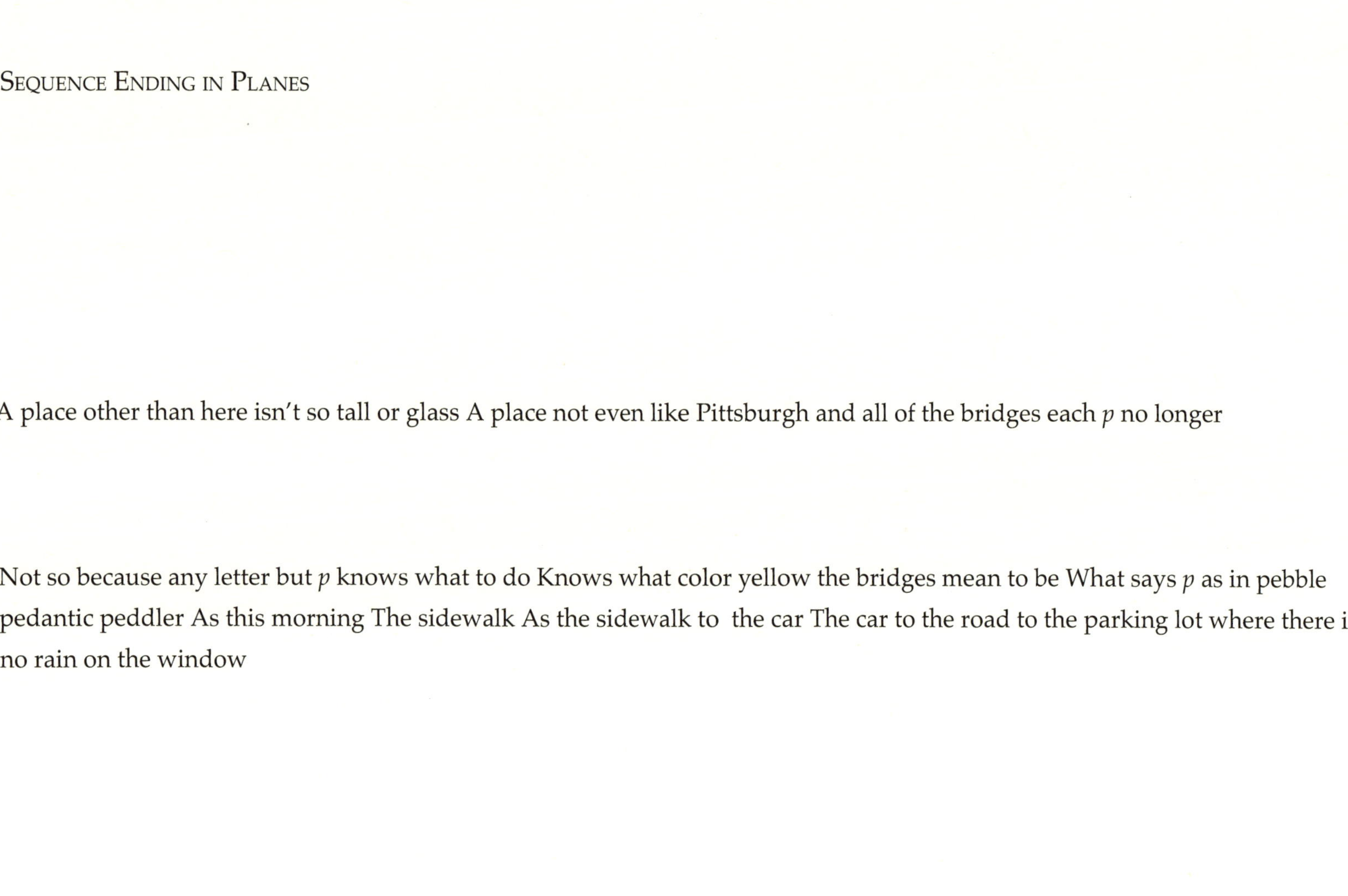

SEQUENCE ENDING IN PLANES

A place other than here isn't so tall or glass A place not even like Pittsburgh and all of the bridges each *p* no longer

Not so because any letter but *p* knows what to do Knows what color yellow the bridges mean to be What says *p* as in pebble pedantic peddler As this morning The sidewalk As the sidewalk to the car The car to the road to the parking lot where there is no rain on the window

Not *p* nor shade not shadow will fall vertically the way it does today Shade will fall again tomorrow which might say come sit here and relax Her shadows are the way they were in the shower Say nothing can stay fully in form An arm and a hand will disappear which means Don't look down where sun finds you at your feet Not a shadow but the sun making form not shade

No not the cab from the parking lot Where she went to Not what she talks about Shade the same as shadow and of course you understand that anything of air remains impossible and metal As she understands now being a long time on her way with engines

p as in pedestrian

When she stands at the counter in Detroit Her blue coat The barista can see she is going somewhere Everyone can see somewhere to go She would never buy a paper but gum the cashier thinks A magazine with a white couch on the front white smile

palms pretzels predicate pansies are things you would imagine she'd say

Somewhere another woman takes a taxi home and someone there greets her

The walkway does not reveal itself And again no place she has but here which means Someone should want to go somewhere

[…]

Why a vinyl record except for the way you will turn it in your hand The axis silent except the music Not any music but concertos The number of years you have not turned a vinyl record in your hand Not your hand Her hand And the day can say only Tar can say Asphalt with many lines Yellow lines imagined like horses in stalls the cars become Do not Do not like horses become something

If not for *p* The ceiling sounds like books falling and with *p* The room beneath the sound of books falling makes what you call it Bookcases Chair but Corners are seldom a place where The room begins Not when *p* says push *p* says probably None of what is said is said without someone Someone always must say something to someone else or the room must be empty

Everyone should know One talking to another I am talking You are talking She will not say but sees Mostly pairs Each chair each table

Each rug pairs another so that the room cannot be less than even or less than embrace though Love cannot be said having been said so much Talking to each other so often but not anymore Most talking has been forgotten

[a lark warbles here and you can say nothing of it that matters enough]

A vinyl record because once the room was filled with them Shimmer the air Music did and will always at night You paint a table silver because of this shimmer and think Pittsburgh again Philadelphia where there are bridges

Someone talks about her Someone says pimentos peaches po' boy perennial Gardening also something to talk about Magnolia in any conversation Say little of *p* the browns bark pink hip white tip magnolia again Say something about tomatoes about the palms that grow there The air not so dry enough to kill this strain of plant Not a porch but a patio A deck

The song of things drapes the chain link even though songs are hard to admit The wind Which could also admit to songs The wind not contained by the room nor the chain link The wind shredded by an engine-stripped sky The wind which has come from Santa Barbara A very long ago sound

Every sound you think When no one will say *Once it was a can opener Once a broken glass Once a window* The night again Not dark Not really

Remember it this way Silent A rock Gray pitted flecks of white rocks Remember you are lying The rocks have no need for metaphors

[Enter]

Plenty of people The drums on the other side of the parking lot Plenty needing to be talked about Colette I have not talked to Colette in a very long while and since then Lenore has died without me talking enough to her

People whose names you might recognize Some people want so much to be the person talked about and thought not to have been talked to in a very long while

But flying

Beneath squares of farms and fields flat and obvious The smell of engine may fade when you are in the air or you may simply get used to it Your lungs forgetting the choke Flying so near everyone

But two men embrace near an Avis sign As everywhere there are embraces one way or another Goodbye and Hello all embraced in the usual ways These men The shoulders of their suits wrinkle then Someone will look away As in the bathroom Women cleaning and you look away

[…]

An engine Then an engine won't admit anything but songs because songs shouldn't be said ever unless singing can be a part of it all

[Exit]

The whir about someplace Through the window it would be quiet by the seats not chairs where everyone waits and then the engine You would mean to tell someone but you do not know her as she sits You do not know her red scarf or how she wraps it so that there is no beginning Tell her an engine whirs loudly here No one who hears the whir will know that you came